Shortcut to Thief River Falls

Shortcut to Thief River Falls

Poems by

Shoshauna Shy

Cover design by Shay Culligan
Cover image by Shoshauna Shy
Author photo by Jeanne Tyree-Francis

ISBN: 979-8-90146-701-5
Library of Congress Control Number: 2026931471

Kelsay Books
502 South 1040 East, A-119
American Fork, Utah 84003
Kelsaybooks.com

To Jim, Taylor, and Jade always

Acknowledgments

Grateful appreciation to the editors of the following journals, e-zines, magazines and anthologies in which these poems appeared, some in slightly modified versions:

Apple Valley Review: "Subsequent Wife"
Aqueous Magazine: "Once They Decided on Divorce"
A Quiet Courage: "Birth Mother"
Autumn Sky Poetry Daily: "White Pickets"
BigCityLit: "What Happened to My Parents After They Gave Me Up"
Black Coffee Review: "Seven Killer Landmines to Botch Your Birth Daughter Reunion"
Blue Hour Magazine: "Hotplate Box from Sears Shows Up"
Briar Cliff Review: "Beautiful Weather"
Cerasus Magazine: "Snipped"
Change Seven: "Blueberries"
Creative Wisconsin: "(No) Return to Sender"
Fish Publishing Poetry Prize Anthology 2021, Finalist: "What My Parents Were Wearing When She Decided Not to Keep Me"
Flash Boulevard: "My Birth Mother Thinks of Me When"
flashGlass: "What My Father Was Doing When He Learned That I Existed"
Flint Hills Review: "Birth Certificate," "The Conversation, Asbury Avenue 1959"
Gulf Stream: "You Join MatchDotCom Two Weeks Before Thanksgiving"
Instant Noodles: "The Ox & Lamb Kept Time"
Little Eagle Re/Verse: "I'm the Future Ex Bill Meets in Saratoga Springs," "Two O'Clock Eureka Joe's"
Local News (anthology): "No Place Like"

Lothlorien Poetry Journal: "The Artist Arrives to Pack Up Her Show, Learns Nothing Sold," "The 'Chosen' Child Chooses," "Homemade from Scratch," "The Thrice-Divorced Woman in the Locker Room Braids Her Hair"

Main Street Rag: "One Thing You Never Want to Learn the Hard Way," "Together Four Decades"

Mentress Moon: "The Week He Asked for a Trial Separation"

Midwest Review: "Silver-Bearded Man in the Waiting Room at the Dental Clinic"

Milk Sugar Literary Journal: "Two O'Clock Eureka Joe's"

Miller's Pond: "Only Child"

Mothers Always Write: "Áfter a Week on Her Turf"

Naugatuck River Review: "Walking Through the Church Where My Husband's Fiancée Got Married"

Naugatuck River Review 15th Annual Contest Anthology 2024, Finalist: "Not Wanting to Meet My Birth Mother"

Northwind Treasury Contest Anthology 2024: "Where to Put Henry"

Not One of Us: "The Adoptee Tells Her Story"

Orange Room Review: "Mr. Morris & Mrs. Wiff Are in Their 80s"

Out of Line: Who Defines? Halfs, Steps, In-Laws & Belonging Anthology: "New Sisters"

Passager 2025 Poetry Contest Anthology, Honorable Mention: "Lucky Timing"

Peninsula Pulse: "The Taunt"

Poetry Breakfast: "Walking Uptown with My Mother"

Poetry South: "Given Up / Not Giving Up"

Red Cedar: "Converting from VHS"

Red Eft Review: "Reunion Registry"

Rockvale Review: "Marriage Proposal @ Age 96," "Birth Records Sealed"

Samsara Quarterly: "The Week He Asked for a Trial Separation"

San Pedro River Review: "Shared Blood"

Sliver of Stone: "A Former Boyfriend's Son Calls to Talk to My Daughter"

Stoneboat: "I'm the Future Ex Bill Meets in Saratoga Springs"

Storyteller Poetry Review: "Artist's Retreat on the Island," "Marriage Proposal @ Age 93," "Mr. Morris & Mrs. Wiff Are in Their 80s," "The Novelist Goes to a Poetry Reading," "Secret to a Long Marriage," "A Form of Fame"

Taproot Literary Review: "The Week He Asked for a Trial Separation"

Third Wednesday: "Fidelity"

Verse Virtual: "Christmas Eve at the New Girlfriend's House," "Given Up For," "In Our Mid-Fifties, It's Payback Time," "I'm the Future Ex Bill Meets in Saratoga Springs," "Marriage Proposal @ Age 93," "Mr. Morris & Mrs. Wiff Are in Their 80s," "No Encore," "Silver-Bearded Man in the Waiting Room at the Dental Clinic," "Summer Rain," "Tidings of Comfort & Joy"

Write City Magazine; The Write City Review, Vol IV: "The Thrice-Divorced Woman in the Locker Room Braids Her Hair"

Your Daily Poem: "Marriage Proposal @ Age 98," "Mr. Morris & Mrs. Wiff Are in Their 80s," "After a Week on Her Turf"

"(No) Return to Sender" was shortlisted for the Northwind Writing Award 2024 and the Fish Publishing Poetry Prize 2025, then won Second Place in the Wisconsin Writers Association's Jade Ring Contest 2025

Other Books by or Co-Edited by Shoshauna Shy

Cat Sitter Secrets Guidebook
Woodrow Hall Editions (2023)

The Splash of Easy Laughter
Kelsay Books (2017)

The Park & Pleasure Drive
Jewel in Madison's Crown
Woodrow Hall Editions (2014)

Echolocations
poets map Madison
Co-edited with Wendy Vardaman
and Sarah Sadie
of Cowfeather Press (2013)

What the Postcard Didn't Say
Zelda Wilde Publishing (2007)

White Horses On Sale for a Song
Parallel Press (2005)

Lake Wingra Morning
Poems Selected and Edited
by Woodrow Hall Editions (2003)

Slide Into Light: Poems of the Brighter Moments
Moon Journal Press (2001)

Souped-Up on the Must-Drive Syndrome
Pudding House Publications (2000)

Contents

6. *book in the one-buck bin*

1.

small boulders, like doorstops,
don't prop doors open

The Adoptee Tells Her Story

I elbowed in
on their flirtation,
their catch-as-catch-can
drunken immersion
one night in September
on a silver lake.
I was the spark
not stomped to ash;
the wind lifting curtains
that knocked over the lamp;
the party crasher no one
wanted to bounce.
I slid down a shortcut
to Thief River Falls

until eviction, a lay-off,
a bout of colic
conspired to give me
the boot.

The Conversation, Asbury Avenue 1959

My mother informed me
that my first best friend,
the five-year-old next door
        with whom I did cartwheels,
        traded Jujubes and Chuckles,
        called for yard-to-yard
was adopted.
There was such a thing?
Children were movable,
removable, interchangeable?
Was this why Mary Sarah
had no brothers nor sisters,
looked like neither parent
way older than mine;
why her residence in a bedroom
wallpapered with roses
seemed incidental?
As if there were a clause
in a 3-ply contract:
Subject to revocation
upon due cause

Shared Blood

My birth mother a not-chosen bride,
the reason she gave me up,
her “steady” marrying the other girl
slated to birth his child
three months sooner.
Not only did my mother lose
a contest she didn’t know existed,
but who she thought she was to him
evaporated like dew on cat whiskers.
She learned of his upcoming nuptials
from a newspaper column, their smiles
a crystal gleam center page.
Or from her own mother’s mouth,
consonants snapping like flags
in a subzero wind.
From a neighbor over the fence
whose pursed lips scolded.
My father once the family darling
demoted to *scoundrel* having relegated her
to a darker hall of shame before he
skated off to complete a different triangle.
And there I was—corralled, captive, every
molecule of blood pumped through me
by the muscle that kept my mother alive:
her heart in anguish.

Homemade from Scratch

"If you don't mind my asking"
are six words you do mind
and so does your mother.
The asker knows this but asks
anyway, these asking mothers
who crop up on the playground
while you're in the sandbox,
on see-saws, on pony swings.
"Is she really yours?" That adverb
like gravel under your tongue
grows into a boulder, blots out
the playscape, trees and all,
the implication *Where did you*
get her? and *Why did you have to?*
because of course every mom
prefers homemade.
Just like store-bought cookies
are not what you bring
to the Easter brunch potluck.
You're still pre-K so your mother
stalls and falters; she's not practiced
at this and some things cannot ever
be prepped or rehearsed such as when

Mrs. Clegg in the fourth-grade classroom
hands out shiny worksheets, draws with
chalk on the blackboard where the names
are to go for your family tree

and Harriet B. Jiles at the desk next to yours
claims this is for those "with a *Real* family"
then helps herself to the crayolas
you both have to share, takes the one
with the sharpest point.

I Spend Winter Weekends Watching Reruns of *The Waltons*

To be a "chosen child" means you were
un-chosen by someone with whom you
belonged, the substitute serving as stand-in
chosen by an agency (picture a wedding planner
moving name tags on a reception hall sketch)
while of all the players in the choosing, the only entity
given no choice whatsoever is the one up for grabs.
This ensures that the burden becomes yours
to reassure everybody else in their choosing;
to reinforce, realign those high hopes they had
whenever they next get stained or tainted
by doubt, as will happen, over and over,
in quiet ways too numerous to count.
Do this knowing full well, if given a reason
of any kind, the designated "stand-in" mother
could elect to un-choose you too.
This happened once already, did it not?
Yes, this is something she could do.

The "Chosen" Child Chooses

The "Given Up": Practical Tools
for the Adoptee handbook
claims I am accustomed
to inhabiting the lead role
in a mystery novel: *Who*
did this and why?
I studied bus stop mothers
with their grade school children
who mimicked them in gesture,
took affection for granted, said
"My mom won't let me" with pride.
In her summery cottons
with yellow ribbon that circled
a saucy straw hat, Elly's mom
was my choice, always waved with
a smile. I decided me and Elly, due
to a nurse's mischief, got swapped
at St. Luke's, Elly really meant
to belong to Mrs. Chaken
who avoided the bus stop, never
wore blue jeans, stayed homebound
on Show-the-Parents Night.
And now, two decades later,
a letter from some stranger
declaring *she's* my mother,
wants to meet at Colectivo
in downstate Clark County
when it's Elly's mom I adopted
in that fifth-grade fantasy,
an allegiance not outgrown
looped taut like yellow ribbon.

(No) Return to Sender

When you're adopted, the appearance
of envelopes with unmarked photos inside
tugs you into days of rehearsing different
combinations of verbs, adverbs, pronouns

to unleash during the ride to school or in
the bakery aisle at Winthrup's Stop & Shop
to a grown-up who has proven that despite
holding all the winning cards, they are not
about to place them on display.

He or she might put you on display in hand-
knitted cardigans boasting reindeers, give you
bananas sliced into pinwheels, allowance for
dish duty, but when it comes to facts
and figures and all the many *who what whys*

up goes that cyclone fence that won't bend
even when you curl both hands over the links
and shake. Envelopes, plain white ones,
with photos of bare-legged children on tricycles,
men wearing flannel shirts, wives with ponytails

slide out of a basement desk drawer or surface
from a hatbox on a closet floor or arrive
in the mail addressed to the household
by surname without a note, an explanation
or return address so you invent farmhouses

for them—waffle breakfasts before the harvesting
of hay, or jungle gym whoops between orange
Popsicles in backyards where cocker spaniels chase,
hating the carrier for not bringing a sequel,

the machine that smeared the clue of a postmark,
wondering how to recover those consonants
and vowels, locate the place of its starting origin,
what route will allow your return.

Birth Certificate

Born at “Hospital.”
Delivered by “Doctor,”
this substitute form
a generic stand-in,
the original with my
true parents’ names
under seal, sequestered,
shielded by proxy.
Rules, regulations, lips
stretched over teeth
lined up as straight as
a white picket fence.
The courts, the clerks,
all my fake family elders
with whom I was slotted
unite to keep me corralled
by secrets.
Small boulders, like doorstops,
don’t prop doors open

but are placed as wedges
to keep them shut.
“You look nothing like
your mom,” my new friend
says when I get dropped off
at the sixth-grade party.

From then on, I ask Mom
not to drop me anywhere;
don’t invite friends home.

And this sheet of paper
located from a desk
in the grown-ups’ study
bears no names, no signatures,
all clues omitted, renders me
untethered as if never born.

Birth Mother

Her letter arrives in the morning
mail, blue envelope postmarked
Shiloh, Tennessee. Addressed not
to me—you pluck it from my hands,
race upstairs to the sanctum
of *Girl, Sixteen.*
Now this stranger's photo sits
flanked by white tapers, their wicks
burnt black against your windowpane—
For My Alyssa At Last
penciled on the back, her smile
magnetized by your searchlight's beam.
In a room for months sealed

against my tread, stealth your steadfast
to-the-collar companion, finally delivered
this testimony that proves

your face echoes the face
of another woman.
You are truly a daughter.

Birth Records Sealed

I laid my lifelong imprint beneath layers
of his fishable memories, those that included
a Hershey bar at age three, perhaps, galoshes stuck
in mud, a carousel pony. Images surfacing
throughout his teens when writing school essays
or during night awakenings or when facing a therapist
who helps him explore why he hates leaving
the embrace of a shower or his own birthday
or waiting in doorways for a ride.
My faint soapy citrus smell mixed with perspiration
remains embedded in his cerebral folds while

well-meaning adults sketch, fashion, spoon-feed
the same scripted stories intended to shape him
away from me, that early history everybody rewrites.
Yet his first five minutes will always be mine.
I held my baby *first.*

What My Parents Were Wearing When She Decided Not to Keep Me

Mostly black gabardine, her hair freshly trimmed, highlighted; stilettos gleaming. She held her briefcase in one hand the entire time. His trench coat unfastened, a fringe of hair overlapping the collar. A wedding band.

Her sweatshirt said *Save the Chubby Unicorns,* the hood up because it was misting, and she didn't want her hair to frizz. His flannel shirt and Levi's were from Farm & Fleet. Not because he drove tractors or smoked dope, but that was what Great-Aunt Lindy gave him at Christmas, thinking teenage boys dressed like that no matter what decade they were in.

Nothing. Unless you count the strip of sisal and turquoise around her ankle. They were skinny-dipping at Crater Lake because some undergrad threw a party. She planned to tell him she was three months late when they returned to the bonfire. But he swam out to the floating dock with two Bud Lights harnessed to his back, and the redhead from Colorado Springs.

A bridal gown. She was getting married none too soon to a man she knew did not (and would not) ever want children. The Control Top pantyhose didn't fool her sister. He was hiking the Neahkahnie Trail in northern Oregon, muddy cargo pants with maps in the pockets, and a bandana rolled to keep the hair off his face.

A hospital gown. A fresh one for Day Two. Sweaty hair clasped to her crown with a beaded barrette shaped like a butterfly. I can't picture my father because she never knew who was who. Too dark to see all their faces.

Celtic tweeds, sweaters woven on the Aran Islands, matching bracelets of leather threaded with silver. It was a huge mistake. They've been looking for me ever since.

Given Up / Not Giving Up

All those years making a tight circle
to some doorbell ringing
—John Gallaher

In a brick duplex on Klickitat Street
in Portland as I brush my hair.
At a stately Colonial in Cleveland
where I'm flipping pancakes.
In a farmhouse on a dirt road
in Nova Scotia.
I am on a weekend jaunt—I am at
a business conference—I am visiting
someone's aunt allowing Google Maps
to signal another app to track me, one
of my antenna arcing away from the clatter
of kitchen conversation for a footfall
on the porch, an unexpected knock
just after the cupcakes are served.
Believing in serendipity, I also ride
trolleys to the French Quarter in New
Orleans and scan all the female faces
of a specific age bracket, and when
standing in line at La Guardia, study
the incoming passengers.

First it's the limber red-haired ladies
under forty, then as I go gray, it's the more
creased women with longer skirts
and shorter heels.
Surely she is looking for me, too—
has been—from school playgrounds
to city Christmas concerts to commuter
trains out of the Chicago Loop, haunted—
this mother of mine—by what she did
that day we first met.

What My Father Was Doing When He Learned That I Existed

Hopping onto the Dakota B bus as he read a text after a chemistry exam, and the woman he considered a one-night stand was asking him to meet her at Planned Parenthood

Packing for a fishing trip with his buddies when his girlfriend showed up with a three-page letter she received in the mail from his ex-fiancée

Drinking a toast to his bride in a reception hall when my mother appeared in the doorway, stomach round as a beach ball

Decorating a Christmas tree when the TV cut to a breaking story on the local news about a baby left in a bicycle basket outside the fire station, which reminded him of an ultimatum he got last spring, and so he does the math

Pushing his six-year-old twins on swings while scrolling through an email from a cousin asking didn't he date a Sarah-What's-Her-Name at Cane Ridge High? *Well, the reason she left for Iowa early senior year . . .*

Arguing with his eldest sister in a law office over their parents' estate which included a bequest to some grandchild he'd never heard of

Fanning himself with a program while seated in midday heat at his grandson's college commencement when a semi familiar woman sidles up and introduces herself, points me out across the lawn

Reunion Registry

Methodist Social Services sends mention
my maternal grandmother suffered
with arthritis, died of diverticulitis,
but there is nothing more.
The adoption agency's report lists
my mother's age, height, color of hair
at time of relinquishment.
The Adoptees' Association tells me to
petition juvenile court for sealed records.
Instead, I fly the under-radar route, apply
to reunion registries, hope my arrow
of request makes data slide into one
vertical slot proving a half-sibling, nephew
by marriage or cousin-once-removed—
even a shirttail one—stretched their bow
and hit mine.
But within a month, all spinning stops.
Triplicate replies stack up and form
a buttress: *No Matches Found.*
My mother, my father, singly or together
leapt like deer into a tamarack woods
gone golden with sundown in September,
to their ongoing ready-made lives, to
other children they cherish.

What Happened to My Parents After They Gave Me Up

She met her true soulmate under a beach umbrella on Nantucket Island, felt like she *dodged a bullet,* but eventually Soulmate returned to his wife

He took up with a Finnish bricklayer who already had custody of a couple of kids, and neither of them ever came around to liking him

She inherited a yacht and properties on multiple South Sea islands, and didn't want to be anchored to anyone—until she fell for another skipper. Their baby was stillborn.

He swore off romance altogether, and hurled himself into getting patents for his various medical devices that would help save children in refugee camps; caught COVID-19; withered to nothing

She moved to Zanzibar with a man well past his prime and his patience who had a slew of bratty grandchildren

He shambled from one co-mingling to another, convinced the next lady on eharmony would be *the* one, but by the time they met, that one was infertile

She haunted grade-school playgrounds throughout the Sun Belt, imagining there I was and there I was and there I was

They got back together by August, wedded on a mountaintop, had three more daughters

My Birth Mother Thinks of Me When

the girl next door turns five, and all her party
guests arrive dressed like garden fairies, ballet
dancers and princesses

her phone rings several days in a row, and Caller
ID says "Restricted" and no one speaks when
she answers

she dates a divorcé who never invites her to his
apartment when his daughters come for the
weekend

she miscarries that one and that one and that one

her first husband leaves because he doesn't want
to die before becoming a father

her second ex is the one her sons say they rather
spend the summer with "because he's more
fun"

her first son is gay, and her second son marries a
woman who doesn't like her one iota

she moves alone to Gulf Shores and rereads the
letter I sent two decades before that she never
acknowledged

it is the 5th of June—for 1,440 excruciating
minutes

In the Limbo of Maybe

I'm a substitute, stand-in, placeholder-adoptee;
at best a Plan B, at worst a charlatan, recruited
to plump up holiday cards, occupy a place setting,
fill the back seat, serve as admission to the PTO.
But had I never gotten yanked from one woman's stage,
might I be on a walk with stair-step sisters or seated
on a lap in this glacier park train station, brothers
clustered at our feet?

Last I knew, she waitressed IHOPS

overheard at my high school graduation; how she
went on to marry, have other daughters whose names
were flowers that grow on the plains.
I studied maps by Rand McNally, sprung all I'd saved
on motels and gasoline, hitting pancake diners from
Texas to Montana asking cashiers to recognize
her photo, one scored from a desk drawer
ransacked on the sly.
I lean toward the twin peaks of December and July

when arms, like windows, are thrown open in welcome.
Dwell in the taut limbo of *almost* and *maybe:*

she meant to keep me
he was late for my birth
regrets sickened them both

enough to keep looking because it's never too late
to rescue a mistake, double-back on a detour, strive
for amends. So that next tweet or DM or email
I click on, the text or fat letter, the phone call late
at night could return me to my rightful position:

cherished firstborn and the eldest of seven, that
lady's child or that one or that one, C notes
vibrating between two guitars, molecules of blood
matching in recognition and I lift free this layer
gone loose and a-flap, uncover a message finally arrived—

Perhaps   Perhaps   Perhaps

Given Up For

With the aim to counterbalance
the cloak of severed shame
in the years of unwed mothers
(fishing pokes at sleep-overs:
Did your real mama ditch you?;
the holidays with “sibs”
whom you look nothing like;
jokes about Cherokee mailmen
to explain your raven braids),
the Birth Certificate access,
Contact Preference forms,
Mutual Consent registries

although there is no antidote
to the unmentionable *déjá vu*
after you do locate Birth Mom,
that timid lady who
so wanted to be found, it seemed.
Brought you around to family,
a picnic, Laven Beach—then skid
like a car on subzero snow
clean out of your reach

Not here her husband tells you
Hawaii for the winter
or was it to real daughters
raised on Everyday Island?
The holidays stretch week to week
in a cloud of pale silence
familiar as the cardigan
you pick up and tug back on.

I Don't Show Up So You Will Never Call Again

I suggested Colectivo, the neighborhood
living room corner of Sprague and Blair
where the tables are tight so we can
listen in on other conversations when
we don't know what to say ourselves,
when our separate islands of awkwardness
bump up against each other like rowboats
without oars.
There's the danger you look exactly like
your father. Or an ugly version of me,
my features elongated, exaggerated so
they don't fit together as well.
Can't predict which'll be worse.
And what do I order to munch on?
Not an egg biscuit; those require focus
so I don't lose half of it every time I bite.
Lost my appetite the day you called anyway.
A cigarette's all I really want but nobody smokes
in coffeehouses even though a Lucky Strike
was made for this kind of situation: Birth Mother
Receives Reunion Request from Son.
Snap on my bulletproof vest for the inevitable
slings and arrows. Why did I say yes?
OK—a cup of tea. Can't stand the taste,
but hey, it'll provide my hands with something
to do. Or for solace, a fudge brownie?

They sell them there, stick walnut bits in them.
Except that will mean reliving what could manifest
as an hour of misery any time I eat another one.
Why risk killing future joy? But I could stand
to shed sixty pounds, Lord knows. 6-0 pounds.
Getting turned off by chocolate might help, ha ha.
Not a bad diet plan. Speaking of which—how big
are you? Am I going to be embarrassed to be seen
with you? Or embarrassed that you see what's
become of me? Damn. What *has* become of me?
I don't like this. I don't like the idea of this
at all.

White Pickets

Of course I tell
my birth mother
in a letter I spend
three years composing
on different colors
of stationery trying
out different inks
(pink too childish,
red too bossy), *I had*
a wonderful upbringing
which is what you are
supposed to say when
you finally locate yours

so she doesn't think
you carry a grudge
nor are you seeking
an apology, just asking
write me back some
thing anything please

and so mine does informing
me her beloved husband
never knew and *Let's keep it*
that way.

With this one penciled
sentence on a half sheet
of note paper, a snapshot
of a lanky girl with blonde
ponytail wearing culottes
straddling a bicycle behind
a white picket fence.
Sandals white. Teeth white.
The number 12 written on
the back with the present year.
She looks a lot like I did once.

Enough said.
This baby she kept.
Daughter of husband.
No trespassers allowed.

Seven Killer Landmines to Botch Your Birth Daughter Reunion

Admit your other children (the ones you kept) know nothing about her, and forget to include the word "yet"

Shrug as if you have no regrets which will show you are too dense to understand she knows you're lying

Conversely, say giving her up was the worst day of your life, which will not elicit sympathy, for who wants to be the cause of someone's worst day of their life?

Yap about the family vacation to Sarasota Springs last week, one more reminder of another adventure you had without her

Curse her father; claim he was a worthless SOB and "You don't need to hear about him" which is another way of saying you get to have firsthand knowledge of an important person she was cheated out of knowing

Gush "You were better off without me." To what end are you trying to convince her of something you don't believe yourself?

Blurting "Good thing you got my profile!" is not the gal-to-gal glue you think it is when she decides to show you a photo of her adoptive mother

Not Wanting to Meet My Birth Mother

means not wanting her to show me
the photos of should-have-been-sisters,
my actual grandpas, a bevy of cousins
clustered in barnyards with strawberry
shortcakes in a katydid August, no space
for me on the heirloom glider, no bourbon-
smoked chicken at picnic tables, donkey
tail parties, stars strung on trees.
I imagined my mother slept in pin curls,
wore gingham dresses, wore linoleum out
between sink and stove top; did not confess
her transgression to friends after returning
in eight months "from Aunt Jan's in Illinois."
I pictured her married to a dairy farmer
as a no-nonsense wife hanging bedsheets
on the line, shoveling dirt for marigold gardens,
belting out babies in stair-step fashion the better
to forget her very first.

Now at the far side of eighty-five, immobilized
in a narrow hospice bed, she requests by mail
I finally arrive, as if that could top off the foaming
milk bucket, erase decades of mutual nonstop
hunger, snip every split end gone gray and frayed

while I rather keep her corralled in Kansas,
contained back there in the 1950s, squeezing
clothespins and pie crusts and canning tongs,
wearing sensible shoes.

2.

daughters in cleveland bathtubs cry

Walking Uptown with My Mother

Me 10 or 11 stumbling along
in my stained Hush Puppies
while she collects catcalls
from workmen in passing trucks
like posies plucked and pocketed
for safekeeping, my mother in a

corduroy A-line miniskirt, boots
knee-high Nancy Sinatra-style, hair
left loose to swing down her back
in blonde curls.
She did not acknowledge this fanfare,
smile nor wave, but her shoulders
got straighter, heels lifted higher

and when we got home, she pulled
those whistles out to wear every time
she passed one of our hallway mirrors.

Blueberries

I expected the note: *Laurie, I left*
for Tulsa. Be good because she'd
warned Dad of that all year.
Each morning I got up in dread
she'd left us and then wishing
she had when I saw her staring
out the window and she wouldn't say
a thing to me except *Don't forget*
you got Scouts after school.
She wasn't even with us when she
put supper on the table, indifference
and boredom in the meatloaf she
didn't eat, smoking her Marlboros
and sipping Folgers instead.
Her note to me was anchored by
a cup of blueberries she'd bought
that day especially for me,
little baubles gleaming still wet
from a rinse of water, the last bit
of motherness she managed.

The Ox & Lamb Kept Time

No martyr me
pulling into the office parking lot
between Christmas and New Years,
the only moving car in probably
a five-mile radius.
That's because many eggnog-sodden souls
are rolling over on Kansas City sofas
to the sound of children arguing,
and wish they could do exactly what I am.
Plenty of twenty-something upstarts
sit at breakfast tables in Duluth
marooned without their Cinnabon-
&-espresso after giving up on
getting a word in edgewise
with Aunt Gladys.
I'm warming up the copier

as midlife men wish for release
from Sis's plan for *how-we-shall-bond-*
over-cocoa-and-Parcheesi
and hubbys sneak down into Winnetka
rec rooms to check email before wives
happily pawn them off to Mayberry Mall
with Grandma Shiskin.
Daughters in Cleveland bathtubs cry
trying to brace themselves for a debate
about who should *not* get the back forty
that Dad left in August, and here am I:

orphaned, divorced and child-free
dunking fudge into a cup of hot coffee
and listening to my Mac boot *ho ho ho,*
the fax *fa la la,* the shredder *pa-rum-pum-*
pum-pum

The Taunt

How apropos
that forever you'll wear
proof of the impulsive wrath
you awakened in your nemesis
and mentor. A milky sliver

risen to seal the cut in flesh
now smooth as ice, a slice
of star, sharp as your tongue,
your face's testimony to
a pane of glass, a ball, a brother.

Hotplate Box from Sears Shows Up

on the porch; the slide-chain
on his bedroom door to keep
his mother out; deadbolt to keep
out me; the weeks stacking end
to end where we don't see him—just
dirty plates on attic stairs, T-shirts
down the laundry chute, on the landing
sandy boots.
Skip calls from school overlap
our voice mail; we strip them off
like layers of paint.
The circling overhead when we settle
at bedtime; showers 3 a.m.
with the radio's bleat;
me straining for a glimpse
of his face at Star Cinema;
Jan sure she spots him
on a park bench
Christmas Eve.

Only Child

They kept the bedroom
at the end of the hall
the way she had left it
fifteen years before
when the runaway horse
collided with hers:

Mary Poppins pressed open
to page eleven, canvas shoe lying
on its bright tassel, bedcover tossed
across peppermint sheets—

as if she were in the upper pasture
and all it would take to bring her back home
was simply a soft summer rain

Converting from VHS

One of those storefronts
you don't ordinarily notice
like they deliberately don't want
to show up on any radar,
plastic sign sagging
where an awning should be
sandwiched between
the Tar Lounge and a highway.
If only you hadn't spent
two quarters of an hour
trying to locate the place,
wife cursing beside you,
but here you are—
better make the best of it,
your little cardboard box
with daughter's dimpled
childhood tucked under
your arm. There's a dusty
card table, a pair of folding
chairs, a few empty Coke
bottles and a bony character
who shuffles slowly towards you.

How do I not do this
doesn't even cross your mind
as much as *How soon can I*
leave while this rickety figure
fingers your precious cargo.

You climb back into the car
wondering if you'll ever find
this shop a second time
or if you do, will the windows
be papered over—worse yet,
will you get a call claiming

these tapes are long gone
unless you drop 5K
at Shank Corners by midnight?

After a Week on Her Turf

If you have to leave your daughter
in her adopted town
2000 miles or more from the city
where you live, and this means
a flight with a Denver stopover

book it for early or midafternoon
so that breakfast is at leisure
in a sun-striped dining room
where a sprig of cherry blossoms
frame a window that shows
a road stretching to the mountains.
In your bowls are strawberries

while her hoop earrings swing
with a shine that echoes
the glint in her eyes.
She wears brand-new jeans,
hiking shoes for scuffy trails,
a sweater blue as sky,
and is planning a walk, upon
your departure, down the hill
to get papayas for lunch.

And if you depart
while the day is still young
it will make it easier than leaving
cloaked by the night
when you stare down from the plane
at the lights' spreading glitter
and she but a single one
somewhere amongst them all

In Our Mid-Fifties, It's Payback Time

My last word of this game
he was confident of winning
trumps the fact he had inched
thirty points ahead,
my possession of the letters
transformed his verb   E X I T E D
which he did not notice
till it was his turn and there

I'd won sixty amazing points
for my adjective E L A T E D
depositing me feet first
in the champion corner
which helped make up for all those
long afternoons of childhood
when he got to pole-vault
to the house-of-seven-sons,
he the brother with admission rights
while I stayed stuck at home—too young,

too dumb, too stupid G I R L
to follow.

Where to Put Henry

Crafting the obituary
for their widowed mother
in her final days,
the eldest daughter omits
mention of Henry, the gent
whom their mother accompanied
everywhere, and who passed
away the week before.
But the youngest son, who shot
pool with Henry on Sunday
afternoons in the community room,
insists Henry should be included.
The eldest son winces.
Sides with sister.
No way.
The youngest daughter sides
with younger brother; thinks
it's OK as long as the sentence
with Henry's name doesn't touch
the sentence that mentions Dad.
The middle daughter suggests tagging
Henry on at the end of the paragraph
listing great-grandchildren where it
won't stick out.

The youngest son says they could
call Henry her "boyfriend"
but somebody who's 90+ is many miles

from boyhood, so how about
"subsequent suitor"?

The middle son says nobody uses
"suitor" in this century, and besides,
Henry was not that either.
This makes the middle daughter blurt
did you not know Henry proposed

to Mom on her 97th birthday?
All jaws drop.
The eldest son insists Henry was simply
the neighbor.
The youngest shakes his head. Claims
he was more like "beloved companion."
The middle daughter points out
they can't say beloved; they mention Dad
and don't call *him* that.
The middle son says I know what
I can call him.
The eldest daughter says let's drop it,
OK? Mom won't know either way
and *The Aurora Sun Times* charges
by the inch.

She goes down the hall to check
on their mother in the far bedroom,
finds her fast asleep.

The framed 8x10 of a jovial Henry
in dapper cap and parka, once
positioned on her nightstand,
is folded to her breast with both hands.
Eyes burning, the daughter returns
to her sibs. Hearing her footfall,
they lift expectant faces.

Henry gets his own paragraph,
she announces.

3.

high noon sun,
never warm enough

Summer Rain

I am fourteen and the first boy
to kiss me on a porch in summer rain
will dump me, only I don't know
that yet. When exiled across
Lake Michigan due to my parents'
vacation to Mexico, I'll seat myself
cross-legged in a field of Queen
Anne's Lace and write a letter
to him while he is back home
kissing my best friend.
When I return, all telephones
will ring unclaimed in hushed
houses, windows will be painted
shut, the high noon sun, never
warm enough.
Forty years later, he will tell me
he remembers receiving my letter

and I will understand, at last,
the plight of Faithful Flora
surviving on the pixie dust
of memory and promise;
turncoat Karlene enthralled
by her reflection in his eyes;
this teenage boy himself whose
appetite could not be stalled
by a square of inked-up paper.

Crooked Gleam

You don’t want
to be a mere fourteen
when you happen upon
a man like that
’cause you’ll wish your mama
married younger so she
had you sooner
A man like that

can pull your dress off
& you won’t care
if you have to crawl
over the edge of a cliff
in order to get it back
Make you believe
your tongue drips gold
even if you are piss-poor
Convince you that
upbringing you had
belongs to somebody else
It’s suicide to count
on a man like that

when you need to come up
with a truck for your brother
warm milk for the baby
money by midnight

although if you want him
make sure it's when
you aren't married already
or somebody's mom
& not studying to take
the GED for the only way
to manage a man like that

is if you're unemployed
until November
with enough cash
for all the gasoline
& margaritas
you're going to need

You Join MatchDotCom Two Weeks Before Thanksgiving

because orphaned, never wed, not-a-mom,
and estranged from sisters, you would like
to avoid another holiday season spooning
takeout while watching British boys sing
O Tannenbaum on TV, folding towels
at the Suds-O-Rama on Beacham Street
those weekends either side of Christmas
and New Years stretching time shapeless
as a sweater crocheted from dimestore yarn.
Shuttered flat, the whole town leaves you
to rattle around like a marble in a shoebox
wearing sweat pants and mucklucks

when what you want is velvet and stilettos;
you want candlelight and crystal; a place
at a table with flaxen-haired preschoolers
and wizened elders tilting their cups
of egg nog, passing platters laden with ham
while all around ricochets the banter
of stair-step brothers; cousins laughing;
a powdery matriarch with a gentle smile
presiding; backstories supplied in the pantry
sotto voce while helping other wives put away
the good china.

You want to cook French toast and pour
cocoa, referee rounds of Scrabble while
wearing pajamas, attend a party cushioned
by nieces on piano, skate a pond amongst
apple-cheeked toddlers, so what if your date

is a widowed insomniac or a 3 x divorcé as
long as he strings words together like
My sister always   *Uncle Ted believes*
Mom invited and wears clean khakis
with creases, cups your elbow as you climb
over snowbanks to a car

Christmas Eve at the New Girlfriend's Parents' House

Made it through the *We wish you a merry*
whiskey old-fashioned artichoke dip & shrimp
asp *Hark the* humus & deviled eggs + *two*
turtle doves in the crème de menthe and the
what-does-your-father (I don't know) *when-did-*
you-gradu—(never did) *where-are-you-work* (no
place now) then 3 a.m. race from guest room
past her room past their room to the pitch
black bathroom and *whew!* the commode
just as bowel unloads—except

lid's down flat and in it I've sat
O holy night
every towel white as snow

Two O'Clock Eureka Joe's

His cousin arranged this
so he agreed to show up
to find that the 30+ woman
seated beside the ficus plant
has a head of amber curls
which gives her face a spritely
flourish, and he likes how
her sweater sleeves are pushed
to the elbows signifying
a take-charge demeanor.
The woman sees his thick crop
of sun-streaked hair and dark
lashes, but would trade either
for another eight inches in height.
Even six.
Still, his jacket with the loosened
hip buckles and stylish cuffs
makes up for it.

He figures he could excuse
the lack of cleavage if she listens
to Duke Ellington or drives
a newer car.
And after she orders a second
almond steamer, he bets it
could become endearing
the way she pronounces the "t"
in "often."

She gives him the benefit
of the doubt that he doesn't
always tap table tops or rock
a knee (he is simply nervous
as is she), and thinks it charming
the way he tests his latte
with his tongue.

He surmises he could adapt
to the smell of strawberry
shower gel if she enjoys
spending hours in a kitchen.
She hopes his broad palms
indicate an affinity for shovels
and bandsaws, though an aptitude
for engines would be equally
advantageous.
He wonders if she has gotten
a marriage proposal from
anyone yet, and if not, why not.
She wishes he had left his ex-wife
instead of the other way around
because *Krissy* has cropped up
more than is pleasing, and estimates
that 40% of his tone is regret,
60% relief, but it's tricky
to determine.

She is not convinced she wants
a dinner date to follow
and he has no idea that the only way
a dinner date will follow
is if he harnesses his impulse
to suggest it then doesn't contact her
again till Thursday.

When their mugs are near-empty,
the badminton birdie exhausted
between them, and she has given
him a shy little wave outside
before hopping onto a bicycle

he decides that if it turns out
she is partial to Star Trek reruns
and never votes Republican,
he could forgive
the thick ankles.

Snipped

I wanted a son or daughter;
You the avenue.
You heard this and withdrew
Your arm from my waist;
Withdrew your leg from me too.
How you sat up and reached
For the photo in your wallet:
The boy born already that looked
So much like you.
And in those barren months
I existed with your absence

I imagined a woman's hands
As they held you to her breast,
Held a pan of eggs, a vase
Or flour sifter, her hair loosened
From its braid and swinging
Past her shoulder.
Imagined how she walked your boy
On sidewalks home from school,
Gave him Oreos and milk,
Taught him the piano,
Bathed him in a tub,
The washcloth white and blue.
I listened to her everywhere

As she talked about the tulips
Blooming in your yard
While mine did their blooming, too;
Advised me to add rosemary
When I basted chicken;
Turn nightshirts inside out
If hanging them on the line.
But since I learned from the internet

You never were a husband,
Much less someone's father

I miss her, Nick, I miss her more
Than I actually miss you.
This phantom wife you said you had
To cut me out of your picture.

I'm the Future Ex Bill Meets in Saratoga Springs

at a Citgo station.
I am still married
and neither of us suspects
I will become my husband's ex,
then Bill's live-in girlfriend.
Next I'm his almost-fiancée

till drunken hijinks
with his best friend
gets me pregnant.
As things go, I miscarry;
Bill forgives me; we get
back together; we break up.
This goes on for years

while he travels to Key West
and dates someone else's wife.
Meanwhile, I give birth
to a couple of his kids;
we get a license;
we have a wedding,
but before I know it
all hell breaks loose

and I'm his ex, Bill's very own ex.
I figured I was *olly olly in free*
but as Bill says, guy reaches forty,
he's bound to have an ex;
maybe even two.

This makes for a handy excuse
when my successor, a pretty
wannabe-Mrs. named Alyssa
prepares to present her case.
Bill can shake his head

and damn if that's not all it takes
for her to know she should get real
or get gone—it won't get
any better than this.

4.

in this town of braunschweiger breakfasts

Fidelity

The lovers I did not have
play guitar for performance poets,
snowshoe in the Rockies,
pace Chicago el train platforms.
They read novels in Nantucket,
climb ladders in apple orchards,
plant Scotch pines on northern hills,
kayak Colorado.
These lovers I did not have

build Canadian campfires,
bike on the heels of daughters,
swim rivers with red-haired wives.
They're drinking in a tavern
when I'm not at the next table,
laughing at a party to which a brother
does not bring me, riding a train
to Ladysmith I'm not about to board.
My husband makes a toast
to our twenty-three years

and these lovers I did not have
write sonatas for other lovers,
canoe six miles to meet them,
stake a tent in sundown's glow,
have no reason to remember us,
no reason to miss me.

Walking Through the Church Where My Husband's Fiancée Got Married

in this town of heavy haunches
and braunschweiger breakfasts
where dresses and dishcloths
flap on backyard lines,
and steeples face off across
the courthouse lawn.
He became mine

thirty years ago today, and we are
stopping at this sanctuary
where his once-fiancée prayed,
sang psalms through childhood
in cousin-thickened pews,
ribbons sticking to her nape
in humid summer wilt.
My husband runs his hand up

the banister to the balcony,
lavender light washing
through stained glass on his face
as it did those mornings before
passing the boats of gravy
at her parents' dining table
where he auditioned shyly
for permanent admittance,
the last to know he'd seen the last

of those hefty Sunday dinners,
another man to take his seat
set squarely in her future.

A Former Boyfriend's Son Calls
to Talk to My Daughter

for he has somehow become attuned
to her frequency despite their being thrown
into a class of six hundred at the local high school.
I hear him ask for her over the telephone

> and am flung into the mountains of Estill County
> in honeysuckle June with moccasin snakes slapping
> their way through warm and muddy water
> amidst arguments that didn't dissolve in bed or out

certain beyond the shadow of a doubt
that after we make it back home to the Midwest
his will be one voice
I'll never hear again

Lucky Timing

Despite the Alberta clipper
down from Canada, your blood
is warm after the dinner-on-
the-town-for-two when, regardless
of a long marriage with its clammy
weeks of illness, smashed Toyotas,
the beige of a thousand Monday mornings,
you look at your husband of a quarter-
century as he stands before the cashier
paying the bill as if seeing him
for the first time—the worn suéde
jacket, the dapper cap, the elfin tilt
of ears—and realize that if it were now,
just right now when you first crossed
his path, you'd hunger for him with
every molecule thrumming in your body

while he belonged to somebody else,
of course, a husband to somebody
with dainty teeth or a salt-and-pepper
pageboy waiting patiently at his elbow.
Would he even notice you here
in the restaurant lobby?
Maybe a brief nod to you, out of courtesy,
and with that, a corkscrew to your navel,
a dry gulp of longing making it impossible
to breathe before you square your shoulders

and glance backwards over the *real* flush
of years behind you, to that sprig of a girl
climbing the acid rock of the sexual revolution
onto some hangout porch in a college town
where you got your first glimpse of him,
bicycle wheels at his knees and April sun
in his eyes, new to the future as you
and just as ready.

Together Four Decades

Married couple pastime:
taking a walk in that hour
of evening René Magritte coined
"The Empire of Light" while we
psychoanalyze why this couple
engaged five years or that one
married twenty crashed and burned
at the guardrail of the hairpin turn,
smoke billowing.
Like children with rabbits' feet
in clutch as we hopskotch
in the schoolyard, we toss,
retrieve and examine pre-packed
suitcases, cell phone excuses,
the grapevine unearthing
ill-placed kisses that preceded
these breakdowns, as if bad luck,
like secret landmines, were at fault
for lives running amok, as if
trust and choice had nothing
to do with it. As if we, too, were
not tasked, from time to time,

with using both palms to cradle
that golden strand of light, that
guiding flame when it flickers
in the unexpected draft
of summer's breath

New Sisters

They are the fur slippers sought first
Step out of bed, the bookends to your
Holiday weekends, the buffer from
The wider world's clang and concrete,
This bevy of women raised
With your husband.
Wearing cabled cardigans and full-
Throated laughter, they hold your
Babies, play with your children,
Attend their graduations, beam
Through their weddings, comprise
The bedrock, the infrastructure
For your seasons of marriage.

Secret to a Long Marriage

Leaving Home Depot
with a light fixture
for our kitchen

he cracks what he calls
One of my stupid jokes

and even after we cross
the parking lot
I still cannot stop laughing

Scrabble for Breakfast

Search for the vowel to complete
two verbs, the "A" or "I" or "E"
that reads both ways, the noun
cracking options open. Draw
from the shuffle dealt generations
ago, what shook down in this gamble

called marriage. Try to work in concert
so that impulse won't derail the other's
intention, know that the choice to place
a consonant in an open space—a decision
made throughout the children's tantrums
or triumphs—will affect what comes down
the pike, maybe boomerang badly.
We were never sure of reaching
the September finish line intact, that fall
when a U-Haul carts the youngest away

as we had not been certain of advancing—
after that initial court & spark—to the land
of sturdy couples walking Yahara Park
bracketed by babies between mortgage
payment days. Now our house holds only

us for the first time, the dryer tossing
flannels, feet in suéde slippers, Rice Chex
in matching bowls as we taste how, despite
the ragged trades, the adjustments,
rearrangements, concessions and apologies,
every letter fit on the board, after all,
and sun-creased, grayened, we're here
with spoons lifted, pleased to make
the acquaintance of who this is
we have each turned out to be.

Silver-Bearded Man in the Waiting Room at the Dental Clinic

I've never seen him before
but I'd like to look at him
across a breakfast table
while sunshine oranges
a pitcher of juice, a light wind
adds a soundtrack of patio
wind chimes, the young day
at our feet like a sheltie who just
noticed an open gate.
None of this is going to happen,
of course. I will not discover what

games the hayloft or fire hydrant
witnessed in his boyhood summers,
nor in what township he wed
a former sweetheart (her name Gretchen?
Lisa?) and if he hiked the Apostle
Islands on his honeymoon.
I will not learn his nickname bestowed
by his eldest daughter nor the story
of how he earned it, where he found
his dog if he has one, what route
he biked after taking the Merrimac
Ferry toward Baraboo. So, let me savor

the next twenty-seven seconds
seated side-by-side in upholstered
armchairs as *Scarborough Fair*
through ceiling speakers drifts down,
and we wait—together, I pretend—
to get called back for root canals.

Mr. Morris & Mrs. Wiff Are in Their 80s

meeting again
at the grocery store
after he wintered
in San Diego.
Backyard neighbors
decades before & three
funerals later, they trade
suggestions for cinnamon
rolls, updates on great-
grandchildren.
Spend July twilights
on her screened porch,
iced tea from a pitcher.
There are short story
collections to read aloud,
Upword scores to tally,
Netflix rentals of DeNiro
& Streep for they have
rescued one another

from suppers of cereal
spooned over the sink,
telephones draped
in cobwebs, hauntings
by happier holidays;
presented themselves
with sunny bouquets
of *Let's & Would you*
        like to

Marriage Proposal @ Age 93

My mother-in-law
finds seventeen ways
to squeeze mention of him
into an hour's conversation
when we visit in her kitchen
for lemonade and forkfuls
of raspberry crisp
Giddy as a schoolgirl
who just got asked
to go steady by the boy
she's long had a crush on
his name a silver song
the breeze carries through
the screen far sweeter
than summer

Marriage Proposal @ Age 96

They're joyriding again—my
mother-in-law and the man
across the hall whom she met
at the Angel Park potluck.
Daughters forbid she drive
her Buick but he still has his,
and she tells him when it's safe
to accelerate through the yellow
before it goes red.
They picnic on Evergreen Island
if there's a table in the shade,
cruise to the family cabin to catch
sunset on the pier, to her childhood
church and farmstead before brunch
at The Silky Spoon.
As if his were a 50s Skylark
with fins and dog dish hubcaps,
and he wore jeans with the cuffs
rolled up, Lucky Strikes tucked
at his bicep, her cardigan buttoned
like a cape, blonde curls
streaming backwards.
It's a pandemic summer slick
with Purell, but the wind washes
them both clean.
The rosebush they bring to our patio
blooms beyond the season's first frost.

Marriage Proposal @ Age 98

He asks her again—
she ten years widowed
after seven married decades,
her name engraved on a tombstone
where her first husband lies.
Marry me please
this one bringing her peaches,
not wanting to die with no record
of their love.
And love him she does

for his yes-let's-go lightness, dapper
countenance, easy humor, caring
kindness, pious nature.
But she is also fond of their separate
apartments; the freedom for holidays
with her own blood kin;
breakfast at six or maybe 10:30.
Besides, there's that plot
on the other side of town,
someone waiting.

Subsequent Wife

After Ted Hughes

No blank slate,
no bucket all shine,
no beribboned basket.
You don't get a floor
fresh-swept, a clean drawer,
linen white and pressed.
Any honeymoon tour brings
arching necks, whispers half
cradled, the scent of suspicion
even before you appear.
What does *not* remind him

when you leap rock-to-rock
or your skirt hem slides?
She is that dent of regret
in his eyes, the shadow
of the hat brim, the recipe
favored, books splayed
for weeks in morning glare.
And crowded that bed
with children squandered—
plus those who survived
a sleep tonic, curettes.

You roll over and another chest
flattens, more dark ink flows.

I imagine the catch
of your own breath, Carol,
each time you light a stove.

Tidings of Comfort & Joy

Of course money can't buy
a holiday weekend
like dear Winnie and I
used to have.
But if she's thick in the hips
or a dim switch, who cares?
Just want someone who's willing
to let me reminisce.
We'll linger over streusel,
drink eggnog, play piano,
pore over Checkers and Back-
gammon, watch classics on TV.
Laid it out in my ad
for the agency:

> *Widower wants*
> *weekend companion*
> *No strings attached*

so could this be she?
Bus in from Chicago
belching out a lady
skinny as a rail
in clumsy galoshes,
another with her hair
coiled 'round foam rollers
(thank God *not* for me)

and then this one clutches
a small overnighter;
she's stout as a barrel,
lips thin and pinched.

Helena? I approach,
holding out my hand.
Eyes narrow to slits,
and she further stiffens.

You better not be the next
mistake of my life!
barks the glaring biddy,
my merry Christmas wife.

One Thing You Never Want to Learn the Hard Way

Don't place an order for roses
to be sent to your wife
with a card that claims *Darlin'*
I'll do anything you say

at the same time you order
asters for the neighbor
whose cat you ran over
on your bicycle last night
Joni forgive me

5.

in the same way cats
need their tails for balance

The Week He Asked for a Trial Separation

She had not realized
that she had come to relish
the heft of her braid
hanging down her spine
slapping a rhythm on
each cheek of her buttocks
as she jogged the bike route
that met Fairview Lane
How she savored its swing
this rope between shoulders
needing its weight against
the skin of thin shirts
in the same way cats need
their tails for balance

Once They Decided on Divorce

First it was a tent flap.
He whispered to her from one side
and she responded.

Then it was a screen door.
Although she kept her back to him,
she still listened.

Next a storm door.
He had to shout to be heard.
She didn't shout back.

After that, an oaken entry
with a brass knocker and kickplate.
She never answered.

Now it was a bank vault.
Not even their daughter was willing
to carry his messages inside.

The Thrice-Divorced Woman in the Locker Room Braids Her Hair

She's been that surge to merge, the whisk of the
waltz, buttery confections, sizzle and steam; the
comfort of flannel, coffee percolation; the climb
to vertigo, the jump to surrender—lather, rinse
repeat. But is this failure? What else lasts
a lifetime? At least each bond lasted long
enough to matter, just like the seasons
that silken to sweaty, sift over to
snow. A bare foot on the bench
braces for balance as she
separates three bundles:
lift, twine and tug to
the last paintbrush
inch, satin-flat as
her palms press,
no strands astray.
She knows how
to start things.
How to finish
them too.

No Encore

They fought less that Christmas, all of us
applauding Dad's glint-eyed banter, Mom's

    cowboy waffles, the way they duo-glided
    from beribboned room to room, Paddy

hanging off Dad's leg, giddy, robin-
breasted; Jay-Boy's laugh a waterfall

    whatever song he played; Mom herself
    a-shimmer as if savoring a secret nowhere

bright as Dad's, none of us near-guessing
his next act booked to open on someone

    else's stage, the leading lady velvet gloss,
    her sleigh on New Year's snow.

Beautiful Weather

What I have of yours
is my crow's cap of hair,
a penchant for mischief,
the gap between teeth.
All I have to keep
that you once touched

is a postcard of a tropical
shoreline, shot through
the mail slot on my sixth
birthday, the ink rain-blurred,
Barbados the postmark:

You were beautiful
Here is the weather

as Mother cursed, knew I
expected a sequel, saw my
convictions squashed cake
by cake.
Each speck of sand in that
glossy picture I studied
for footprints, but the camera,
like me, was unable to hold you.
I imagined a pirate with gold-
tooth-and-eye-patch beyond
the palm tree under my left
thumb, a better place to put you

than the Kettle Moraine prison
where I heard you slept.
I grabbed memory's snapshots,
pieced a collage: cinnamon
on my tongue, popcorn's buttery
smell, red shiny shoes with bows.

My ribs remembered the support
of your forearm as you carried me,
the warmth of your chest
against shoulder blades.
No voice to replay, no face.
Aunt Satch admitted I was
at the state fair in Gladys Park
with you for one day.
On homework sheets, I rearrange
your words, make them say all
the things you might have written—

You the weather were
Here is beautiful wish

The wish here is you
Were weather beautiful

The weather is beautiful
Wish you were here

No Place Like

Skinny clapboard house
same block as Haskell High
where nobody cared
if I wasn't there by roll call,
so by spring semester,
I didn't go at all.
Just laid on the mattress
Dad stuck in the attic
of that house he had
with Sandy after he left Mom.
I stayed with Mom

till the JB Hunt driver
doing runs to Detroit
started knicknacking her
with trinkets and whiskey.
Dad and Sandy Monday
mornings laughing in the kitchen
with beer cans and stale popcorn
till she drove him in her Camarro
to his shift at the drycleaner's,
and she cashiered at Blistaff's
past dinnertime.
I sat on the front porch waiting
for Tyler to show up with something
to smoke, or pizza from the gas station.

When I return to that Podunk
because it's Easter and Mom asks me,
all of Main Street's shrunken down
to dust and wet cardboard: sunken
Haskell High, Blistaff's faded awnings,
kids' bikes dropped in the mud.

Dad skipped town, someone said,
probably living in Hawaii

while Sandy's Camarro
still sits in the driveway
like it has nowhere to go
even if it gets invited.

6.

book in the one-buck bin

The Novelist Goes to a Poetry Reading

to torture himself.
Secretly, he wishes he were a poet
so that he didn't have an agent
on his back egging him to pay homage
to her bottom line.
And he would be quite happy to rely
on white space to emphasize
his insightful declarations.
The novelist is tired of having to write
pages and pages of prose in order to say
what a poet can say with a few choice words.
To have every syllable matter seems exalting

especially when he is at a stalemate
with his characters who are acting
like they don't care if he finishes the book
without them.
That's when he slinks into Café Montmartre
with its orange lamps and rattan couches
for the deliciously patient hush as
a poet settles at the podium to deliver
her utterances.
The novelist listens to each perfectly
positioned preposition, each adverb
as it pulses in the air, the reverence
that cushions them—

and then those sweet little throat-clucks
the audience makes when they resonate
with the final line.

Artist's Retreat on the Island

The first week featured Ariel,
a weaver from Tel Aviv,
her cabin flanked by willows,
bed double-wide, bowed deep.
The next session presented Gertraud
with her wool skeins from Berlin,
and after that a novelist
from New York named Evelyn.
Sunday afternoons delivered
a fresh crop to the grounds

and Jeremy who taught wood carving
with his touch for symmetry
chose one woman for conversation,
recreation and release.
Someone to smooth his ego,
dig out the burled knots
since he got pitched asunder
by wife *numéro* three.
Long years of faithfulness he gave,
and he'd been played the fool.

While there were rules against gate-crashing
anybody's solitude
as they each cocooned in cabins
with canvas, pen or loom,
Jeremy located one good match who,
primed by his flirtations
welcomed an evening visitor
for masterful diversion.

The best candidates sported wedding bands
and emitted joie de vivre

    so in the fragrant summer woods
    it took little to spark intrigue:
    a lifted brow, a few soft words,
    compliments for creations.
    Becca—Heather—Margueritte
    all tumbled in succession.
    Saturday farewells tender,
    then Sundays found him freshened.

No other summer bested this one
with its succulent rotations
like the platters in the dining hall,
abundance on display.
Jeremy slid melon between his teeth,
winked at Susan and her canapé.

The Artist Arrives to Pack Up Her Show, Learns Nothing Sold

and envies the poet
who happens upon her book
in the one-buck-bin
under a shop awning
with the inscription
she once penned there
on the title page, proof
somebody read it;
somebody once held it
in their hands

A Form of Fame

You are wandering through
a secondhand bookstore
in a town you didn't know
was on any map, population
900, a four-day drive from home
when there on the shelf is one
of your poetry collections,
and the table of contents
is cocoa-stained, some pages
dog-eared, the back cover
slightly bowed.
You buy it for 89 cents
so you can read the words
some stranger scribbled
in the margins.

Notes

Poetry is my partner for life, but I am first and foremost a fiction writer. This is why most of my poems are crafted from the POV of someone else that I know, that I don't know, I want to know or someone I'd never want to know. While there are grains of my own actual life experience in them, very few of these poems, even when written in first person, are from my own POV about "what really happened."

For example, the only autobiographical poem in Section I is the second poem, "The Conversation, Asbury Avenue 1959." That friendship affected me wholescale, as I internalized the experiences my childhood friend was going through due to our close proximity.

The other poems written from the POV of adoptees, birth mothers, and adoptive mothers are wrought fictitiously from whole cloth, inspired in part by those I personally know who were adopted, have adopted, or given their own children up.

About the Author

Shoshauna Shy is the author of poetry collections *Souped-Up on the Must-Drive Syndrome* (Pudding House Publications), *Slide Into Light* (Moon Journal Press), *White Horses on Sale for a Song* (Parallel Press), *What the Postcard Didn't Say* (Zelda Wilde Publishing), and *The Splash of Easy Laughter* (Kelsay Books). The latter two won Outstanding Achievement awards from the Wisconsin Library Association.

In 2023 through 2025, her poems were finalists, shortlisted, or received Honorable Mentions from *Naugatuck River Review* for their 15th Annual narrative contest, Raw Earth Ink's Northwind Writing Awards, Fish Publishing's annual poetry prize, Wisconsin Writers Association's Jade Ring Contest, and Passager Books. Her poems have been made into videos, graced the interior of taxi cabs, and even decorated the hind quarters of city buses.

She is also a flash fiction, short story, and micro-memoir author, founder of the Poetry Jumps Off the Shelf program, Woodrow Hall Editions, and the Woodrow Hall Jumpstart Awards. She lives with her husband in Madison, Wisconsin, and runs a thriving cat care business, experiences which have been captured in a nonfiction guidebook called *Cat Sitter Secrets,* which can be found at CatSitterSecrets.com.

Learn more about Shoshauna at:
PoetryJumpsOfftheShelf.com

www.ingramcontent.com/pod-product-compliance
Lightning Source LLC
LaVergne TN
LVHW020637100826
845148LV00012B/2221

* 9 7 9 8 9 0 1 4 6 7 0 1 5 *